WORDS of GOLD

A Treasury of the Bible's Poetry and Wisdom

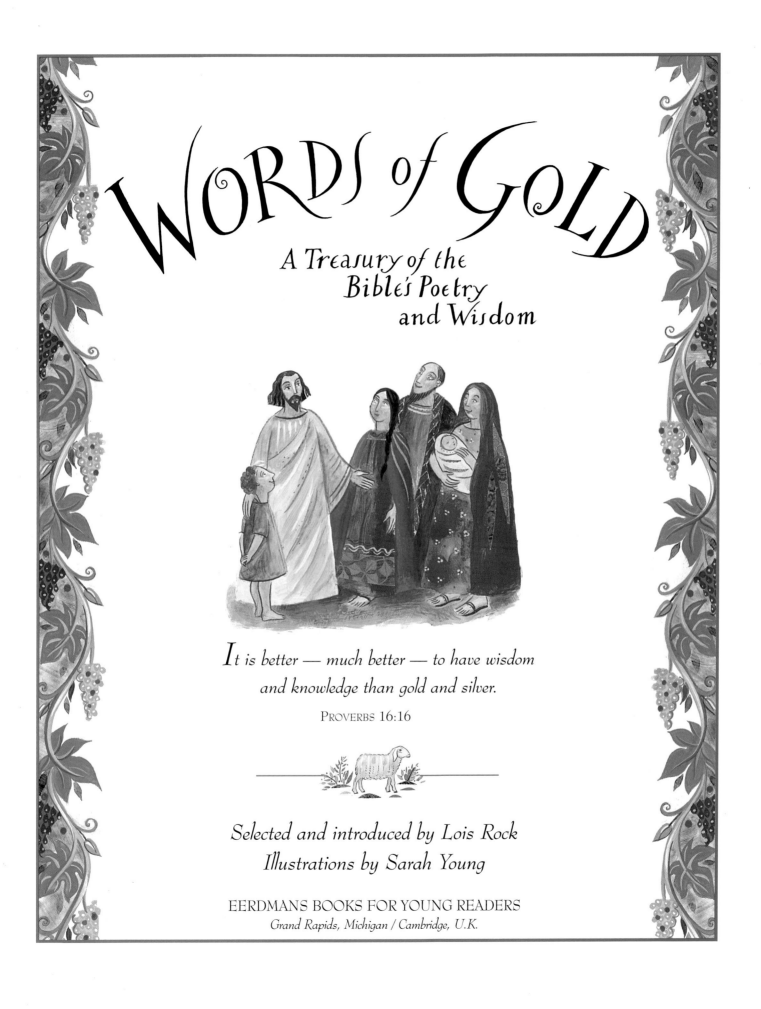

*It is better — much better — to have wisdom
and knowledge than gold and silver.*

PROVERBS 16:16

Selected and introduced by Lois Rock

Illustrations by Sarah Young

EERDMANS BOOKS FOR YOUNG READERS

Grand Rapids, Michigan / Cambridge, U.K.

To Vic, Philip & James

Selected and introduced by Lois Rock
Illustrations copyright © 1997 Sarah Young
Original edition published under the title
Words of Gold: A Treasury of the Bible's Poetry and Wisdom
Copyright © 1997 Lion Publishing plc Oxford, England

This edition published 2000
under license from Lion Publishing by
Eerdmans Books for Young Readers
An imprint of Wm. B. Eerdmans Publishing Company
255 Jefferson Ave. S.E., Grand Rapids, Michigan 49503/
P.O. Box 163, Cambridge CB3 9PU U.K.

05 04 03 02 01 00   7 6 5 4 3 2 1

Acknowledgments
Extracts from the Authorized Version of the Bible (The King
James Bible), the rights of which are vested in the Crown, are
reproduced by permission of the Crown's Patentee, Cambridge
University Press. Scriptures quoted from the *Good News Bible*
published by The Bible Societies/HarperCollins Publishers
Ltd UK © American Bible Society, 1966, 1971, 1976,
1992, 1994 are reproduced by permission. Scripture text
marked NRSV is from the New Revised Standard Version of
the Bible, Anglicized Edition copyright © 1989, 1995 by
the Division of Christian Education of the National Council
of the Churches of Christ in the USA, and is used by
permission.

Library of Congress Cataloging-in-Publication Data
Words of gold: a treasury of the Bible's poetry and wisdom
selected and introduced by Lois Rock;
illustrated by Sarah Young
p.   cm.
Includes index
Summary: Presents passages from both the Old and New
Testaments as lessons on life for children.
ISBN 0-8028-5199-1 (hardcover : alk.paper)
1. Bible Stories, English.[1.Bible--Selections.] I. Rock, Lois,
1953- ill. II. Young, Sarah, 1961-
BS551.2 W63 1999
2209'505 21--dc21
99-037903

Printed and bound in Singapore
Designed by Nicky Jex

Introduction

The Bible is a great storehouse of wisdom for the world.

The word *Bible* often makes people think of the large book that is read slowly and solemnly in cathedrals and churches.

Its origins reveal it in a rather different light. The Bible is a collection of over sixty books. They were put together between two and three thousand years ago, under the bright blue skies of the near East, by the people of Israel.

The writings tell the story of that people: their quest to find a place in this world that they could call home and a way of living that was right and good, honest and fair.

Sometimes life was good for the people: they had flocks of sheep and goats and fertile farmlands carved out of the steep, rocky hillsides.

At other times they found themselves at the mercy of the powerful nations around them. To the south was Egypt; to the north Assyria, Babylon and Persia. From across the Mediterranean came other nations — the Philistines, the Greeks, and finally the Romans. When enemies came marauding the world was harsh and cruel, and the people of Israel wept as they tried to understand what life was all about.

The questions they asked were the questions that people everywhere have always longed to understand: Why does the world exist? What is the purpose of human life? Why is the world sometimes so lovely, and at other times so cruel and unfair? What happens to people when they die? Where can lasting happiness be found?

In their writings, the people of Israel tried to make sense of a puzzling world. They wrote their ancient stories about the beginnings of the world, and their belief in a Creator God who was good and loving. They wrote their history and saw that when they lived as God's people, they were safe, whatever happened around them; when they were cruel and unfair, disaster and despair followed. Their priests and prophets strove to remind them of what God is like, and taught them the things they believed God wanted them to understand.

In the time of the Romans, Jesus was born to the people of Israel. He was the One promised to their people from centuries before, the One who would show the world how to live as God's people, the One they called the Messiah, the Christ. His followers, who became known as Christians, produced new writings to tell the story of Jesus and his message — a message of God's love for the world, and of a secure happiness and peace for all who responded to that love.

In the centuries that followed, all these writings were gathered together. They have been read and pondered for generations.

People find in them something that satisfies their longing to understand the great questions of life — something that brings them courage and joy, wisdom and understanding, and a happiness that nothing can destroy.

Here is a glimpse of some of that wisdom — wisdom that is more precious than gold.

Contents

Stories of the Beginning

Who made the world? Why does the world exist at all?
The Bible begins with ancient stories that give the answers.

In the Beginning

These are the first words in the Bible, the start of a story about how God
made the world in six days and rested on the seventh day.

In the beginning when God created the heavens and the earth, the earth was a formless void and darkness covered the face of the deep, while a wind from God swept over the face of the waters. Then God said, "Let there be light," and there was light. And God saw that the light was good; and God separated the light from the darkness. God called the light Day, and the darkness he called Night. And there was evening and there was morning, the first day.

GENESIS CHAPTER 1, VERSES 1–5, NRSV

Knowing Good and Evil

The Bible says the world God made was good. The first people lived in a garden paradise named Eden. God warned them never to choose evil.
Very soon, however, temptation came.

Now the serpent was more crafty than any other wild animal that the Lord God had made. He said to the woman, "Did God say, 'You shall not eat from any tree in the garden?'" The woman said to the serpent, "We may eat of the fruit of the trees in the garden; but God said, 'You shall not eat of the fruit of the tree that is in the middle of the garden, nor shall you touch it, or you shall die.'" But the serpent said to the woman, "You will not die; for God knows that when you eat of it your eyes will be opened, and you will be like God, knowing good and evil." So when the woman saw that the tree was good for food, and that it was a delight to the eyes, and that the tree was to be desired to make one wise, she took of its fruit and ate; and she also gave some to her husband, who was with her, and he ate.

GENESIS CHAPTER 3, VERSES 1–6, NRSV

Paradise Lost

The Bible tells how when people chose evil the whole world became a harsh and cruel place. People lost their garden paradise.

Then the Lord God said, "See, the man has become like one of us, knowing good and evil; and now, he might reach out his hand and take also from the tree of life, and eat, and live forever" — therefore the Lord God sent him forth from the garden of Eden, to till the ground from which he was taken. He drove out the man; and at the east of the garden of Eden he placed the cherubim, and a sword flaming and turning to guard the way to the tree of life.

GENESIS CHAPTER 3, VERSES 22–24, NRSV

The People of Israel

The Bible tells the history of a people who were special to God: the people of Israel. Their story began long ago, when God chose a man named Abram — later known as Abraham — to be the father of their nation. Through that family, that nation, God made a promise to do good things for everyone in the world.

God's Promise to the World

God made this promise to Abraham and to the world.

The Lord said to Abram, "Leave your country, your relatives, and your father's home, and go to a land that I am going to show you. I will give you many descendants, and they will become a great nation. I will bless you and make your name famous, so that you will be a blessing.
I will bless those who bless you,
But I will curse those who curse you.
And through you I will bless all the nations."

GENESIS CHAPTER 12,
VERSES 1–3, GNB

6

The Stairway to Heaven

The Bible tells how God's promise was passed on to Abraham's son Isaac. One of Isaac's twin sons, Jacob, cheated his brother Esau to get this blessing for himself. Although he was found out and had to run for his life, God was still good to him.

Jacob left Beersheba and started towards Haran. At sunset he came to a holy place and camped there. He lay down to sleep, resting his head on a stone. He dreamed that he saw a stairway reaching from earth to heaven, with angels going up and coming down on it. And there was the Lord standing beside him. "I am the Lord, the God of Abraham and Isaac," he said.
"I will give to you and to your descendants this land on which you are lying. They will be as numerous as the specks of dust on the earth. They will extend their territory in all directions, and through you and your descendants I will bless all the nations. Remember, I will be with you and protect you wherever you go, and I will bring you back to this land. I will not leave you until I have done all that I have promised you."

Genesis chapter 28, verses 10–15, GNB

The Naming of Israel

At the end of Jacob's life, God appeared to him again and blessed him. He then gave the nation the name by which it would be known for generations to come.

God said to him, "Your name is Jacob, but from now on it will be Israel." So God named him Israel. And God said to him, "I am Almighty God. Have many children. Nations will be descended from you, and you will be the ancestor of kings."

Genesis chapter 35, verses 10–11, GNB

Blessings

God continued to do good things for the people of Israel; God continued to bless them. Here is an ancient prayer from the Bible asking for God's blessing.

May the Lord bless you and take care of you;
May the Lord be kind and gracious to you;
May the Lord look on you with favor and give you peace.

Numbers chapter 6, verses 24–26, GNB

The Law of God

*Abraham, Isaac, and Jacob were the great ancestors of the people of Israel.
In Jacob's time, the family moved to Egypt as welcome guests. Many years later,
they became slaves in Egypt. Then God gave them another great leader, Moses.
He led them out of Egypt to a land where they could be free to live as God's people.*

The Ten Commandments

*As the people traveled to freedom in a new land,
God gave them ten great laws,
the Ten Commandments.*

And God spake all these words, saying, I am the Lord thy God, which have brought thee out of the land of Egypt, out of the house of bondage.

Thou shalt have no other gods before me.

Thou shalt not make unto thee any graven image, or any likeness of any thing that is in heaven above, or that is in the earth beneath, or that is in the water under the earth:

Thou shalt not bow down thyself to them, nor serve them: for I the Lord thy God am a jealous God, visiting the iniquity of the fathers upon the children unto the third and fourth generation of them that hate me;

And showing mercy unto thousands of them that love me, and keep my commandments.

Thou shalt not take the name of the Lord thy God in vain; for the Lord will not hold him guiltless that taketh his name in vain.

Remember the sabbath day, to keep it holy.

Six days shalt thou labor, and do all thy work: But the seventh day is the sabbath of the Lord thy God: in it thou shalt not do any work, thou, nor thy son, nor thy daughter, thy manservant, nor thy maidservant, nor thy cattle, nor thy stranger that is within thy gates:

For in six days the Lord made heaven and earth, the sea, and all that in them is, and rested the seventh day: wherefore the Lord blessed the sabbath day, and hallowed it.

Honor thy father and thy mother: that thy days may be long upon the land which the Lord thy God giveth thee.

Thou shalt not kill.

Thou shalt not commit adultery.

Thou shalt not steal.

Thou shalt not bear false witness against thy neighbor.

Thou shalt not covet thy neighbor's house, thou shalt not covet thy neighbor's wife, nor his manservant, nor his maidservant, nor his ox, nor his ass, nor any thing that is thy neighbor's.

Exodus chapter 20, verses 1–17, KJV

Laws of Justice

God also gave the people of Israel other laws to guide them: laws about how to celebrate festivals, how to worship God, how to seek God's forgiveness, along with laws about how to care for their land and show love and justice towards their fellow human beings.

"Do not ill-treat or oppress a foreigner; remember that you were foreigners in Egypt. Do not ill-treat any widow or orphan."

Exodus chapter 22, verses 21–22, GNB

"Show respect for old people and honor them. Reverently obey me; I am the Lord."

Leviticus chapter 19, verse 32, GNB

"Do not take advantage of anyone or rob him. Do not hold back the wages of someone you have hired, not even for one night. Do not curse a deaf man or put something in front of a blind man so as to make him stumble over it. Obey me; I am the Lord your God.

"Do not take revenge on anyone or continue to hate him, but love your neighbor as you love yourself. I am the Lord."

Leviticus chapter 19, verses 13–14 and 18, GNB

"When you harvest your fields, do not cut the corn at the edges of the fields, and do not go back to cut the ears of corn that were left. Do not go back through your vineyard to gather the grapes that were missed or to pick up the grapes that have fallen; leave them for poor people and foreigners. I am the Lord your God."

Leviticus chapter 19, verses 9–10, GNB

Teach the Children Well

"Israel, remember this! The Lord — and the Lord alone — is our God. Love the Lord your God with all your heart, with all your soul, and with all your strength. Never forget these commands that I am giving you today. Teach them to your children. Repeat them when you are at home and when you are away, when you are resting and when you are working."

Deuteronomy chapter 6, verses 4–7, GNB

God Our Defender

Moses brought the people to the edge of the new land which they made their home. They faced many dangers and felt afraid. Were they still God's people? Would God still take care of them? It took hundreds of years for them to understand that when they disobeyed God, disaster followed; when they obeyed God, they were blessed.

God's Promise of Protection

After Moses, a young soldier named Joshua had the task of leading his people into the land and making it their home. God spoke to him:

"No one shall be able to stand against you all the days of your life. As I was with Moses, so I will be with you; I will not fail you or forsake you. Be strong and courageous; for you shall put this people in possession of the land that I swore to their ancestors to give them. Only be strong and very courageous, being careful to act in accordance with all the law that my servant Moses commanded you; do not turn from it to the right hand or to the left, so that you may be successful wherever you go."

JOSHUA CHAPTER 1, VERSES 5–7, NRSV

Defeating Giants

Many years after the time of Joshua, enemies called the Philistines threatened the nation. They knew the secret of making iron weapons that could blunt the dull bronze blades of the Israelites. So how did an Israelite shepherd boy named David win a great victory against the Philistine champion?

Then he [David] took his staff in his hand, and chose five smooth stones from the wadi, and put them in his shepherd's bag, in the pouch; his sling was in his hand, and he drew near to the Philistine.

The Philistine came on and drew near to David, with his shield-bearer in front of him.

When the Philistine looked and saw David, he disdained him, for he was only a youth, ruddy and handsome in appearance. The Philistine said to David, "Am I a dog, that you come to me with sticks?" And the Philistine cursed David by his gods. The Philistine said to David, "Come to me, and I will give your flesh to the birds of the air and to the wild animals of the field." But David said to the Philistine, "You come to me with sword and spear and javelin; but I come to you in the name of the Lord of hosts, the God of the armies of Israel, whom you have defied. This very day the Lord will deliver you into my hand . . . so that all the earth may know that there is a God in Israel, and that all this assembly may know that the Lord does not save by sword and spear; for the battle is the Lord's and he will give you into our hand."

When the Philistine drew nearer to meet David, David ran quickly towards the battle line to meet the Philistine. David put his hand in his bag, took out a stone, slung it, and struck the Philistine on his forehead; the stone sank into his forehead, and he fell face down on the ground.

So David prevailed over the Philistine with a sling and a stone, striking down the Philistine and killing him.

1 SAMUEL CHAPTER 17, VERSES 40–50, ABBREVIATED, NRSV

Restoring the Nation

In spite of all the signs of God's love, the people still failed to trust God. The time came when they were utterly defeated. Many of the survivors were taken to a foreign land. When, at last, they returned, they saw more clearly than ever that God had stayed faithful to them.

And then the people of Israel prayed this prayer: "You, Lord, you alone are Lord; you made the heavens and the stars of the sky. You made land and sea and everything in them; you gave life to all. The heavenly powers bow down and worship you.

"But your people rebelled and disobeyed you; they turned their backs on your Law. They killed the prophets who warned them, who told them to turn back to you. They insulted you time after time, so you let their enemies conquer and rule them. In their trouble they called to you for help, and you answered them from heaven. In your great mercy you sent them leaders who rescued them from their foes."

NEHEMIAH CHAPTER 9, VERSES 6 AND 26–27, GNB

The Way to Wisdom

*The Bible also contains writings from poets, playwrights, and thinkers,
who give advice and say what it means to be wise.*

There are mines where silver is dug;
There are places where gold is refined.
Miners dig iron out of the ground
And melt copper out of the stones.
They explore the deepest darkness.
They search the depths of the earth
And dig for rocks in the darkness.
Far from where anyone lives
Or human feet ever travel,
They dig the shafts of mines.
There they work in loneliness,
Clinging to ropes in the pits.
Food grows out of the earth,
But underneath the same earth
All is torn up and crushed.
The stones of the earth contain sapphires,
And its dust contains gold.
No hawk sees the roads to the mines,
And no vulture ever flies over them.
No lion or other fierce beast
Ever travels those lonely roads.
Miners dig the hardest rocks,
Dig mountains away at their base.
As they tunnel through the rocks,
They discover precious stones.
They dig to the sources of rivers
And bring to light what is hidden.

But where can wisdom be found?
Where can we learn to understand?
Wisdom is not to be found among mortals;
No one knows its true value.
The depths of the oceans and seas
Say that wisdom is not found there.
It cannot be bought with silver or gold.
The finest gold and jewels
Cannot equal its value.

It is worth more than gold,
Than a gold vase or finest glass.
The value of wisdom is more
Than coral or crystal or rubies.
The finest topaz and the purest gold
Cannot compare with the value of wisdom.
Where, then, is the source of wisdom?
Where can we learn to understand?
No living creature can see it,
Not even a bird in flight.
Even death and destruction
Admit they have heard only rumors.

God alone knows the way,
Knows the place where wisdom is found,
Because he sees the ends of the earth,
Sees everything under the sky.
When God gave the wind its power
And determined the size of the sea;
When God decided where the rain
would fall,
And the path that the thunderclouds
travel;
It was then he saw wisdom and tested its
worth —
He gave it his approval.
God said to human beings,
"To be wise, you must have reverence for
the Lord.
To understand, you must turn from evil."

A SPEECH FROM THE STORY OF JOB, WHICH IS WRITTEN AS A PLAY.
JOB CHAPTER 28, GNB

Songs and Prayers

Imagine being able to talk to the One who made the entire universe! Imagine that great One listening.
Here are some of the songs and prayers the people of Israel offered God, the One they called the Lord.

Praise the Maker

The earth is the Lord's and all that is in it, the world, and those who live in it; for he has founded it on the seas, and established it on the rivers.

PSALM 24, VERSES 1–2, NRSV

Praise the Lord of the World

Praise the Lord, all you nations! Extol him, all you peoples! For great is his steadfast love towards us, and the faithfulness of the Lord endures for ever.

PSALM 117, VERSES 1–2, NRSV

God the Protector

The Lord is my shepherd; I shall not want.

He maketh me to lie down in green pastures: he leadeth me beside the still waters.

He restoreth my soul: he leadeth me in the paths of righteousness for his name's sake.

Yea, though I walk through the valley of the shadow of death, I will fear no evil: for thou art with me; thy rod and thy staff they comfort me.

Thou preparest a table before me in the presence of mine enemies: thou anointest my head with oil; my cup runneth over.

Surely goodness and mercy shall follow me all the days of my life: and I will dwell in the house of the Lord forever.

PSALM 23, KJV

Light in the Dark

The Lord is my light and my salvation; whom shall I fear? the Lord is the strength of my life; of whom shall I be afraid?

PSALM 27, VERSE 1, KJV

A Prayer for a New Start

Have mercy upon me, O God, according to thy lovingkindness: according unto the multitude of thy tender mercies blot out my transgressions.

PSALM 51, VERSE 1, KJV

A Nighttime Prayer

I will both lie down and sleep in peace; for you alone, O Lord, make me lie down in safety.

PSALM 4, VERSE 8, NRSV

Good Advice

Who wants advice? Every young generation has always thought it knew better than the old. Every aging generation has wanted to help and advise, to save the young from tears and grief. Here are just a few of the wise sayings of the people of Israel.

Now Just You Listen to Me!

Do what your father tells you, my son, and never forget what your mother taught you. Keep their words with you always, locked in your heart. Their teaching will lead you when you travel, protect you at night, and advise you during the day. Their instructions are a shining light; their correction can teach you how to live.

PROVERBS CHAPTER 6, VERSES 20–23, GNB

Be Fair

Be generous, and you will be prosperous. Help others, and you will be helped.

PROVERBS CHAPTER 11, VERSE 25, GNB

If you oppress poor people, you insult the God who made them; but kindness shown to the poor is an act of worship.

PROVERBS CHAPTER 14, VERSE 31, GNB

Better to eat vegetables with people you love than to eat the finest meat where there is hate.

PROVERBS CHAPTER 15, VERSE 17, GNB

Who's Talking?

Children are fortunate if they have a father who is honest and does what is right.

PROVERBS CHAPTER 20, VERSE 7, GNB

Words

When you tell the truth, justice is done, but lies lead to injustice.

PROVERBS CHAPTER 12, VERSE 17, GNB

Thoughtless words can wound as deeply as any sword, but wisely spoken words can heal.

PROVERBS CHAPTER 12, VERSE 18, GNB

A lie has a short life, but truth lives on forever.

PROVERBS CHAPTER 12, VERSE 19, GNB

No one who gossips can be trusted with a secret, but you can put confidence in someone who is trustworthy.

PROVERBS CHAPTER 11, VERSE 13, GNB

Joy and Sorrow

When hope is crushed, the heart is crushed, but a wish come true fills you with joy.

PROVERBS CHAPTER 13, VERSE 12, GNB

Love and Hate

Hate stirs up trouble, but love overlooks all offenses.

PROVERBS CHAPTER 10, VERSE 12 , GNB

Whom to Trust

It is dangerous to be concerned with what others think of you, but if you trust the Lord, you are safe.

PROVERBS CHAPTER 29, VERSE 25, GNB

A Companion in Sorrow

Does anyone understand when everything seems bleak and hopeless?

A Cry of Despair

The words of the Teacher, the son of David, king in Jerusalem.

Vanity of vanities, says the Teacher, vanity of vanities! All is vanity.

What do people gain from all the toil at which they toil under the sun?

A generation goes, and a generation comes, but the earth remains for ever.

The sun rises and the sun goes down, and hurries to the place where it rises.

The wind blows to the south, and goes round to the north; round and round goes the wind, and on its circuits the wind returns.

All streams run to the sea, but the sea is not full; to the place where the streams flow, there they continue to flow.

All things are wearisome, more than one can express; the eye is not satisfied with seeing, or the ear filled with hearing.

What has been is what will be, and what has been done is what will be done; there is nothing new under the sun.

ECCLESIASTES CHAPTER 1, VERSES 1–9, NRSV

Life is Short

So remember your Creator while you are still young, before those dismal days and years come when you will say, "I don't enjoy life." That is when the light of the sun, the moon, and the stars will grow dim for you, and the rain clouds will never pass away. Then your arms, that have protected you, will tremble, and your legs, now strong, will grow weak. Your teeth will be too few to chew your food, and your eyes too dim to see clearly. Your ears will be deaf to the noise of the street. You will barely be able to hear the mill as it grinds or music as it plays, but even the song of a bird will wake you from sleep. You will be afraid of high places, and walking will be dangerous. Your hair will turn white; you will hardly be able to drag yourself along, and all desire will have gone.

We are going to our final resting place, and then there will be mourning in the streets. The silver chain will snap, and the golden lamp will fall and break; the rope at the well will break, and the water jar will be shattered. Our bodies will return to the dust of the earth, and the breath of life will go back to God, who gave it to us.

Useless, useless, said the Philosopher. It is all useless.

ECCLESIASTES CHAPTER 12, VERSES 1–8, GNB

One Thing to Remember

The end of the matter; all has been heard. Fear God, and keep his commandments; for that is the whole duty of everyone.

ECCLESIASTES CHAPTER 12, VERSE 13, NRSV

Warnings to the Wicked

Sometimes the world seems a wicked place. as if people have chosen the wrong road in life. In Bible times, the people of Israel also did wicked things. From time to time, certain people felt called by God to warn the people about their wrongdoing. These people were known as prophets.

Unfair!

You people hate anyone who challenges injustice and speaks the whole truth in court.

You have oppressed the poor and robbed them of their grain. And so you will not live in the fine stone houses you build or drink wine from the beautiful vineyards you plant.

I know how terrible your sins are and how many crimes you have committed. You persecute good people, take bribes, and prevent the poor from getting justice in the courts.

And so, keeping quiet in such evil times is the clever thing to do!

Make it your aim to do what is right, not what is evil, so that you may live. Then the Lord God Almighty really will be with you, as you claim he is.

AMOS CHAPTER 5, VERSES 10–14, GNB

Wicked, Wicked People

The Lord has an accusation to bring against the people who live in this land. Listen, Israel, to what he says: "There is no faithfulness or love in the land, and the people do not acknowledge me as God. They make promises and break them; they lie, murder, steal, and commit adultery. Crimes increase, and there is one murder after another. And so the land will dry up, and everything that lives on it will die. All the animals and birds, and even the fish, will die."

HOSEA CHAPTER 4, VERSES 1–3, GNB

The Wrong Road

The Lord told me to say to his people, "When someone falls down, doesn't he get back up? If someone misses the road, doesn't he turn back? Why then, my people, do you turn away from me without ever turning back? Not one of you has been sorry for his wickedness; not one of you has asked, 'What have I done wrong?' Everyone keeps on going his own way, like a horse rushing into battle. Even storks know when it is time to return; doves, swallows, and thrushes know when it is time to migrate. But, my people, you do not know the laws by which I rule you."

Jeremiah chapter 8, verses 4–7, abbreviated, GNB

A Promise of Good Things

When people find they are traveling in the wrong direction, they can do something about it: stop, turn round, and go back to the right road. In the same way, the prophets of Bible times promised the people that they could turn from wrongdoing and choose once again to live as God's people.

Come Back!

The Lord says,

"I will bring my people back to me.

I will love them with all my heart; no longer am I angry with them.

I will be to the people of Israel like rain in a dry land.

They will blossom like flowers; they will be firmly rooted like the trees of Lebanon.

They will be alive with new growth, and beautiful like olive trees.

They will be fragrant like the cedars of Lebanon.

Once again they will live under my protection.

They will grow corn and be fruitful like a vineyard."

Hosea chapter 14, verses 4–7, GNB

Change Your Ways

"Remove the chains of oppression and the yoke of injustice, and let the oppressed go free. Share your food with the hungry and open your homes to the homeless poor. Give clothes to those who have nothing to wear, and do not refuse to help your own relatives.

"If you put an end to oppression, to every gesture of contempt, and to every evil word; if you give food to the hungry and satisfy those who are in need, then the darkness around you will turn to the brightness of noon. And I will always guide you and satisfy you with good things. I will keep you strong and well. You will be like a garden that has plenty of water, like a spring of water that never runs dry. Your people will rebuild what has long been in ruins, building again on the old foundations. You will be known as the people who rebuilt the walls, who restored the ruined houses."

ISAIAH CHAPTER 58, VERSES 6–7 AND 9–12, GNB

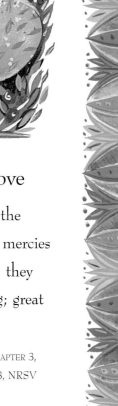

Unfailing Love

The steadfast love of the Lord never ceases, his mercies never come to an end; they are new every morning; great is your faithfulness.

LAMENTATIONS CHAPTER 3, VERSES 22–23, NRSV

In Need of Rescue

*Over the centuries, the people of Israel failed to live as God's people. They knew the laws;
they knew that their God was on the side of all that is good and right. Yet they kept doing wrong
things and forgetting God. Like people trapped in a dark and awful place, they needed someone to
rescue them. The prophets told them that someday God would send
a special king to be their rescuer: a king even greater than the great King David of long ago.
Their word for someone who was chosen by God to be a king was Messiah,
and they were waiting for a Messiah to be born.*

A New King

The royal line of David is like a tree that has been cut down; but just as new branches sprout from a stump, so a new king will arise from among David's descendants.

The spirit of the Lord will give him wisdom, and the knowledge and skill to rule his people.

He will know the Lord's will and honor him, and find pleasure in obeying him.

He will not judge by appearance or hearsay; he will judge the poor fairly and defend the rights of the helpless.

At his command the people will be punished, and evil persons will die.

He will rule his people with justice and integrity.

Wolves and sheep will live together in peace, and leopards will lie down with young goats.

Calves and lion cubs will feed together, and little children will take care of them.

Cows and bears will eat together, and their calves and cubs will lie down in peace.

Lions will eat straw as cattle do.

Even a baby will not be harmed if it plays near a poisonous snake.

On Zion, God's sacred hill, there will be nothing harmful or evil.

The land will be as full of knowledge of the Lord as the seas are full of water.

ISAIAH CHAPTER 11, VERSES 1–9, GNB

Rescued from the Darkness

The people who walked in darkness have seen a great light; those who lived in a land of deep darkness — on them light has shined.

For a child has been born for us, a son given to us; authority rests upon his shoulders; and he is named Wonderful Counselor, Mighty God, Everlasting Father, Prince of Peace.

His authority shall grow continually, and there shall be endless peace for the throne of David and his kingdom. He will establish and uphold it with justice and with righteousness from this time onwards and forevermore.

Isaiah chapter 9, verses 2 and 6–7, NRSV

The Good Shepherd

The Sovereign Lord is coming to rule with power, bringing with him the people he has rescued.

He will take care of his flock like a shepherd; he will gather the lambs together and carry them in his arms; he will gently lead their mothers.

Isaiah chapter 40, verses 10–11, GNB

Is this God's King?

The people of Israel were still longing for the special king from God, the Messiah. Then a young man from Galilee began traveling around the country telling people what he understood about God, and about how people could live as part of God's kingdom. His name was Jesus.

From the beginning Jesus' mother Mary knew her child was special.

The Angel Gabriel Speaks to Mary

The angel said to her, "Don't be afraid, Mary; God has been gracious to you. You will become pregnant and give birth to a son, and you will name him Jesus. He will be great and will be called the Son of the Most High God. The Lord God will make him a king, as his ancestor David was, and he will be the king of the descendants of Jacob forever; his kingdom will never end!"

LUKE CHAPTER 1, VERSES 30–33, GNB

Mary Accepts God's Call

And Mary said, My soul doth magnify the Lord,

And my spirit hath rejoiced in God my Saviour.

For he hath regarded the low estate of his handmaiden: for, behold, from henceforth all generations shall call me blessed.

For he that is mighty hath done to me great things; and holy is his name.

And his mercy is on them that fear him from generation to generation.

He hath showed strength with his arm; he hath scattered the proud in the imagination of their hearts.

He hath put down the mighty from their seats, and exalted them of low degree.

He hath filled the hungry with good things; and the rich he hath sent empty away.

He hath helped his servant Israel, in remembrance of his mercy;

As he spake to our fathers, to Abraham, and to his seed forever.

MARY'S SONG IS OFTEN CALLED *THE MAGNIFICAT,* FROM THE WORD IN THE FIRST LINE. LUKE CHAPTER 1, VERSES 46–55, KJV

The Angels and the Shepherds

*The night Jesus was born
angels told the news.*

And there were in the same country shepherds abiding in the field, keeping watch over their flock by night.

And, lo, the angel of the Lord came upon them, and the glory of the Lord shone round about them: and they were sore afraid.

And the angel said unto them, Fear not: for, behold, I bring you good tidings of great joy, which shall be to all people.

For unto you is born this day in the city of David a Saviour, which is Christ the Lord.

And this shall be a sign unto you; Ye shall find the babe wrapped in swaddling clothes, lying in a manger.

And suddenly there was with the angel a multitude of the heavenly host praising God, and saying,

Glory to God in the highest, and on earth peace, good will toward men.

<small>The angels say that Jesus is *Christ*, this is another word for *Messiah*. Luke chapter 2, verses 8–14, KJV</small>

A Happy Ending

*An old man named Simeon saw the baby
Jesus and knew he was the Messiah.
After seeing Jesus, Simeon said
he now could die happy.*

Lord, now lettest thou thy servant depart in peace, according to thy word:

For mine eyes have seen thy salvation,

Which thou hast prepared before the face of all people;

A light to lighten the Gentiles, and the glory of thy people Israel.

<small>Luke chapter 2, verses 29–32, KJV</small>

God's Welcome

*Jesus had an important message for all people: God welcomes them.
God is greater than the greatest king, yet he welcomes all people
into a very special kingdom. Jesus often told stories called parables
to explain what his kingdom is like.*

The Parable of the Pharisee
and the Tax Collector

He [Jesus] also told this parable to some who trusted in themselves that they
were righteous and regarded others with contempt: "Two men went up to the
temple to pray, one a Pharisee and the other a tax collector. The Pharisee,
standing by himself, was praying thus, 'God, I thank you that I am not like
other people: thieves, rogues, adulterers, or even like this tax collector. I fast
twice a week; I give a tenth of all my income.' But the tax collector, standing
far off, would not even look up to heaven, but was beating his breast and
saying, 'God, be merciful to me, a sinner!' I tell you, this
man went down to his home justified rather
than the other; for all who exalt
themselves will be humbled, but all who
humble themselves will be exalted."

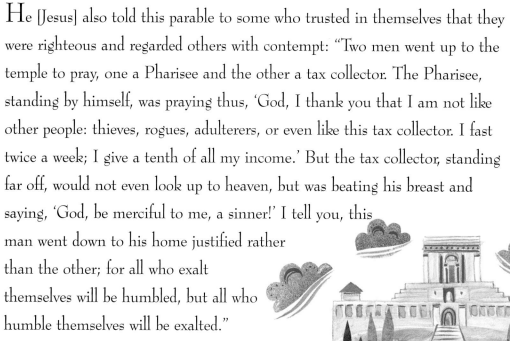

LUKE CHAPTER 18, VERSES 9–14, NRSV

Jesus and Little Children

People were bringing even infants to him that he might touch them; and when the disciples saw it, they sternly ordered them not to do it. But Jesus called for them and said, "Let the little children come to me, and do not stop them; for it is to such as these that the kingdom of God belongs. Truly I tell you, whoever does not receive the kingdom of God as a little child will never enter it."

Luke chapter 18, verses 15–17, NRSV

"See that you don't despise any of these little ones. Their angels in heaven, I tell you, are always in the presence of my Father in heaven.

"What do you think a man does who has a hundred sheep and one of them gets lost? He will leave the other ninety-nine grazing on the hillside and go and look for the lost sheep. When he finds it, I tell you, he feels far happier over this one sheep than over the ninety-nine that did not get lost. In just the same way your Father in heaven does not want any of these little ones to be lost."

Matthew chapter 18, verses 10–14, GNB

The Parable of the Mustard Seed

Jesus told them another parable: "The Kingdom of heaven is like this. A man takes a mustard seed and sows it in his field. It is the smallest of all seeds, but when it grows up, it is the biggest of all plants. It becomes a tree, so that birds come and make their nests in its branches."

Matthew chapter 13, verses 31–32, GNB

29

Learning to Love

How should people live their lives?

The Greatest Commandment

*Once a teacher of the Jewish law asked
Jesus what was the greatest commandment
God had given.*

Jesus said unto him, Thou shalt love the Lord
thy God with all thy heart, and with all thy
soul, and with all thy mind.

This is the first and great commandment.

And the second is like unto it, Thou shalt
love thy neighbor as thyself.

On these two commandments hang all the
law and the prophets.

MATTHEW CHAPTER 22, VERSES 37–40, KJV

Do Not Condemn

"Do not judge others, and God
will not judge you; do not
condemn others, and God will not
condemn you; forgive others, and
God will forgive you."

LUKE CHAPTER 6, VERSE 37, GNB

Freely Forgive

Then came Peter to him, and
said, Lord, how oft shall my
brother sin against me, and I
forgive him? Till seven times?

Jesus saith unto him, I say not
unto thee, Until seven times: but,
Until seventy times seven.

MATTHEW CHAPTER 18, VERSES 21–22, KJV

Love Your Enemies

Jesus taught the people who gathered round him:

Ye have heard that it hath been said, Thou shalt love thy neighbor, and hate thine enemy.

But I say unto you, Love your enemies, bless them that curse you, do good to them that hate you, and pray for them which despitefully use you, and persecute you;

That ye may be the children of your Father which is in heaven: for he maketh his sun to rise on the evil and on the good, and sendeth rain on the just and on the unjust.

MATTHEW CHAPTER 5, VERSES 43–45, KJV

A New Commandment

One evening when Jesus and his special friends, his disciples, gathered to celebrate a religious festival, Jesus did the work of a servant, washing the travel-weary feet of his disciples. Having set this example, he said these words:

A new commandment I give unto you, That ye love one another; as I have loved you, that ye also love one another. By this shall all men know that ye are my disciples, if ye have love one to another.

JOHN CHAPTER 13, VERSES 34–35, KJV

Learning to be Fair

In this world, some have great wealth: others suffer great poverty.
Is this what God wants?
What should people do when they see injustice?

True Riches

Here is what Jesus said:

Lay not up for yourselves treasures upon earth, where moth and rust doth corrupt, and where thieves break through and steal:

But lay up for yourselves treasures in heaven, where neither moth nor rust doth corrupt, and where thieves do not break through nor steal:

For where your treasure is, there will your heart be also.

"No one can serve two masters; for a slave will either hate the one and love the other, or be devoted to the one and despise the other. You cannot serve God and wealth.

"Therefore I tell you, do not worry about your life, what you will eat or what you will drink, or about your body, what you will wear. Is not life more than food, and the body more than clothing? Look at the birds of the air; they neither sow nor reap nor gather into barns, and yet your heavenly Father feeds them. Are you not of more value than they? And can any of you by worrying add a single hour to your span of life? And why do you worry about clothing?

Consider the lilies of the field, how they grow; they neither toil nor spin, yet I tell you, even Solomon in all his glory was not clothed like one of these. But if God so clothes the grass of the field, which is alive today and tomorrow is thrown into the oven, will he not much more clothe you — you of little faith? Therefore do not worry, saying, 'What will we eat?' or 'What will we drink?' or 'What will we wear?' For it is the Gentiles who strive for all these things; and indeed your heavenly Father knows that you need all these things. But strive first for the kingdom of God and his righteousness, and all these things will be given to you as well.

"So do not worry about tomorrow, for tomorrow will bring worries of its own. Today's trouble is enough for today."

Matthew chapter 6, verses 19–21, KJV and 24–34, NRSV

The Widow's Gift

As Jesus sat near the temple treasury, he watched the people as they dropped in their money. Many rich men dropped in a lot of money; then a poor widow came along and dropped in two little copper coins, worth about a penny. He called his disciples together and said to them, "I tell you that this poor widow put more in the offering box than all the others. For the others put in what they had to spare of their riches; but she, poor as she is, put in all she had — she gave all she had to live on."

Mark chapter 12, verses 41–44, GNB

The Lure of Riches

Then Jesus said to his disciples, "Truly I tell you, it will be hard for a rich person to enter the kingdom of heaven. Again I tell you, it is easier for a camel to go through the eye of a needle than for someone who is rich to enter the kingdom of God."

Matthew chapter 19, verses 23–24, NRSV

A New Life

*Jesus called people to follow him. They would live happy lives,
knowing they were at peace with God.*

True Happiness: A Teaching from Jesus' Sermon on the Mount

*Whom will God bless? For whom will God do good things?
Here is what Jesus said:*

And seeing the multitudes, he went up into a mountain: and when he was set, his disciples came unto him:

And he opened his mouth, and taught them, saying,

Blessed are the poor in spirit: for theirs is the kingdom of heaven.

Blessed are they that mourn: for they shall be comforted.

Blessed are the meek: for they shall inherit the earth.

Blessed are they which do hunger and thirst after righteousness: for they shall be filled.

Blessed are the merciful: for they shall obtain mercy.

Blessed are the pure in heart: for they shall see God.

Blessed are the peacemakers: for they shall be called the children of God.

Blessed are they which are persecuted for righteousness' sake: for theirs is the kingdom of heaven.

Blessed are ye, when men shall revile you, and persecute you, and shall say all manner of evil against you falsely, for my sake.

Rejoice, and be exceeding glad: for great is your reward in heaven: for so persecuted they the prophets which were before you.

Matthew chapter 5, verses 1–12, KJV

Praying to God

Jesus told people to build their friendship with God
by praying to God in the right way.

"But when you pray, go to your room, close the door, and pray to your Father, who is unseen. And your Father, who sees what you do in private, will reward you.

"When you pray, do not use a lot of meaningless words, as the pagans do, who think that their gods will hear them because their prayers are long. Do not be like them. Your Father already knows what you need before you ask him."

MATTHEW CHAPTER 6, VERSES 6–8, GNB

After this manner therefore pray ye: Our Father which art in heaven, Hallowed be thy name.

Thy kingdom come. Thy will be done in earth, as it is in heaven.

Give us this day our daily bread.

And forgive us our debts, as we forgive our debtors.

And lead us not into temptation, but deliver us from evil: For thine is the kingdom, and the power, and the glory, forever. Amen.

MATTHEW CHAPTER 6, VERSES 9–13, KJV

Two Houses

"Everyone then who hears these words of mine and acts on them will be like a wise man who built his house on rock. The rain fell, the floods came, and the winds blew and beat on that house, but it did not fall, because it had been founded on rock. And everyone who hears these words of mine and does not act on them will be like a foolish man who built his house on sand."

MATTHEW CHAPTER 7, VERSES 24–26, NRSV

The Last Enemy

Everyone fears death. Death breaks up families and tears friends apart. No one can escape. Death came when people spoiled God's good world. Can anything defeat death? Jesus came and endured the fear, the pain, and the darkness of death.

God's Love

A close friend of Jesus named John knew Jesus was God's son, come to rescue the world from death.

For God so loved the world, that he gave his only begotten Son, that whosoever believeth in him should not perish, but have everlasting life.

JOHN CHAPTER 3, VERSE 16, KJV

The Good Shepherd

Jesus predicted that he was going to die as part of his work of rescuing people from darkness.

"I am the good shepherd. The good shepherd lays down his life for the sheep.

"I am the good shepherd. I know my own and my own know me, just as the Father knows me and I know the Father. And I lay down my life for the sheep. I have other sheep that do not belong to this fold. I must bring them also, and they will listen to my voice. So there will be one flock, one shepherd. For this reason the Father loves me, because I lay down my life in order to take it up again."

JOHN CHAPTER 10, VERSES 11 AND 14–17, NRSV

Jesus Is Put to Death

Jesus soon found his life in danger. Among his own people were those who hated him for the things he said about God. They did not believe he was God's son, the Messiah. They told lies about him to get him into trouble with the governor of the land, a Roman named Pontius Pilate.

Pilate called together the chief priests, the leaders, and the people, and said to them, "You brought this man to me and said that he was misleading the people. Now, I have examined him here in your presence, and I have not found him guilty of any of the crimes you accuse him of. Nor did Herod find him guilty, for he sent him back to us. There is nothing this man has done to deserve death. So I will have him whipped and let him go."

It was the custom that at every Passover Festival the governor had to set free one prisoner for the people.

The whole crowd cried out, "Kill him! Set Barabbas free for us!" (Barabbas had been put in prison for a riot that had taken place in the city, and for murder.)

Pilate wanted to set Jesus free, so he appealed to the crowd again. But they shouted back, "Crucify him! Crucify him!"

Two other men, both of them criminals, were also led out to be put to death with Jesus. When they came to the place called *The Skull*, they crucified Jesus there, and the two criminals, one on his right and the other on his left. Jesus said, "Forgive them, Father! They don't know what they are doing."

They divided his clothes among themselves by throwing dice.

It was about twelve o'clock when the sun stopped shining and darkness covered the whole country until three o'clock; and the curtain hanging in the Temple was torn in two. Jesus cried out in a loud voice, "Father! In your hands I place my spirit!" He said this and died.

There was a man named Joseph from Arimathea, a town in Judea. He was a good and honorable man, who was waiting for the coming of the Kingdom of God. Although he was a member of the Council, he had not agreed with their decision and action. He went into the presence of Pilate and asked for the body of Jesus. Then he took the body down, wrapped it in a linen sheet, and placed it in a tomb which had been dug out of solid rock and which had never been used. It was Friday, and the Sabbath was about to begin.

The women who had followed Jesus from Galilee went with Joseph and saw the tomb and how Jesus' body was placed in it. Then they went back home and prepared the spices and perfumes for the body.

On the Sabbath they rested, as the Law commanded.

LUKE CHAPTER 23, VERSES 13–21, 32–34, 44–46
AND 50–56, GNB

Jesus Is Risen

*At the center of the news about Jesus is one astonishing belief:
Jesus who was crucified rose from the dead.
By rising from the dead, Jesus opened the way for people to live as
members of God's kingdom not just in this life but forever.*

Jesus' Promise

*Jesus knew that he had to die. He knew that this was part of God's
plan to open the way for all people to live as God's friends. This is
what he said to his friends a few hours before he was arrested:*

Let not your heart be troubled: ye believe in God, believe also in me.

In my Father's house are many mansions: if it were not so, I would have told you. I go to prepare a place for you.

And if I go and prepare a place for you, I will come again, and receive you unto myself; that where I am, there ye may be also.

And whither I go ye know, and the way ye know.

Thomas saith unto him, Lord, we know not whither thou goest; and how can we know the way?

Jesus saith unto him, I am the way, the truth, and the life: no man cometh unto the Father, but by me.

"Peace I leave with you; my peace I give to you. I do not give to you as the world gives. Do not let your hearts be troubled, and do not let them be afraid. You heard me say to you, 'I am going away, and I am coming to you.' If you loved me, you would rejoice that I am going to the Father, because the Father is greater than I."

JOHN CHAPTER 14, VERSES 1–6, KJV AND 27–28, NRSV

The Resurrection

But on the first day of the week, at early dawn, they came to the tomb, taking the spices that they had prepared. They found the stone rolled away from the tomb, but when they went in, they did not find the body. While they were perplexed about this, suddenly two men in dazzling clothes stood beside them. The women were terrified and bowed their faces to the ground, but the men said to them, "Why do you look for the living among the dead? He is not here, but has risen. Remember how he told you, while he was still in Galilee, that the Son of Man must be handed over to sinners, and be crucified, and on the third day rise again."

LUKE CHAPTER 24, VERSES 1–7, NRSV

News to Change the World

Rumors were flying around that Jesus was alive. If he really was alive, then all he had said about God's kingdom must be true.

Jesus Appears to his Friends

When Jesus' closest followers, the disciples, began to hear these reports that Jesus was alive, they were unsure what to think.

While they were talking about this, Jesus himself stood among them and said to them, "Peace be with you." They were startled and terrified, and thought that they were seeing a ghost. He said to them, "Why are you frightened, and why do doubts arise in your hearts? Look at my hands and my feet; see that it is I myself. Touch me and see; for a ghost does not have flesh and bones as you see that I have." And when he had said this, he showed them his hands and his feet. While in their joy they were disbelieving and still wondering, he said to them, "Have you anything here to eat?" They gave him a piece of broiled fish, and he took it and ate in their presence.

Then he opened their minds to understand the scriptures, and he said to them, "Thus it is written, that the Messiah is to suffer and to rise from the dead on the third day, and that repentance and forgiveness of sins is to be proclaimed in his name to all nations, beginning from Jerusalem. You are witnesses of these things."

LUKE CHAPTER 24, VERSES 36–43 AND 45–48, NRSV

Peter Speaks to the Crowds
in Jerusalem

After Jesus' resurrection his friends saw him taken up to heaven. Shortly after, something special happened, just as Jesus had promised. The disciples heard a rushing wind and saw flames above their heads, and then God gave them the help and courage they needed to spread the news about Jesus — the message that anyone was welcome in God's kingdom. They all went out into the streets of Jerusalem full of joy, telling the news.

"God has raised this very Jesus from death, and we are all witnesses to this fact. He has been raised to the right-hand side of God, his Father, and has received from him the Holy Spirit, as he had promised. What you now see and hear is his gift that he has poured out on us.

"All the people of Israel, then, are to know for sure that this Jesus, whom you crucified, is the

one that God has made Lord and Messiah!"

When the people heard this, they were deeply troubled and said to Peter and the other apostles, "What shall we do, brothers?"

Peter said to them, "Each one of you must turn away from your sins and be baptized in the name of Jesus Christ, so that your sins will be forgiven; and you will receive God's gift, the Holy Spirit. For God's promise was made to you and your children, and to all who are far away — all whom the Lord our God calls to himself."

ACTS CHAPTER 2, VERSES 32–33 AND 36–39, GNB

New Life as God's People

A man named Paul was at first unconvinced. But God spoke to him in a dramatic way — with a blinding flash of light and a voice from heaven. Then he, too, became a follower of Jesus Christ, a Christian.

Paul Writes a Letter About his Christian Faith

The Good News was promised long ago by God through his prophets, as written in the Holy Scriptures. It is about his Son, our Lord Jesus Christ: as to his humanity, he was born a descendant of David; as to his divine holiness, he was shown with great power to be the Son of God by being raised from death.

I have complete confidence in the gospel; it is God's power to save all who believe, first the Jews and also the Gentiles. For the gospel reveals how God puts people right with himself: it is through faith from beginning to end. As the scripture says, "The person who is put right with God through faith shall live."

ROMANS CHAPTER 1, VERSES 2–4 AND 16–17, GNB

More of Paul's Letter

In view of all this, what can we say? If God is for us, who can be against us? Certainly not God, who did not even keep back his own Son, but offered him for us all! He gave us his Son — will he not also freely give us all things? Who will accuse God's chosen people? God himself declares them not guilty! Who, then, will condemn them? Not Christ Jesus, who died, or rather, who was raised to life and is at the right-hand side of God, pleading with him for us! Who, then, can separate us from the love of Christ? Can trouble do it, or hardship or persecution or hunger or poverty or danger or death?

No, in all these things we have complete victory through him who loved us! For I am certain that nothing can separate us from his love: neither death nor life, neither angels nor other heavenly rulers or powers, neither the present nor the future, neither the world above nor the world below — there is nothing in all creation that will ever be able to separate us from the love of God which is ours through Christ Jesus our Lord.

ROMANS CHAPTER 8, VERSES 31–35 AND 37–39, GNB

Living the Faith

People who believe Jesus is the Messiah, or as the Greek word put it,
the Christ, are known as Christians. Their lives must shine with joy
and goodness.

Rejoice!

Rejoice in the Lord always; again
I will say, Rejoice.

PHILIPPIANS CHAPTER 4, VERSE 4 , NRSV

Led by God's Spirit

What I say is this: let the Spirit direct
your lives.

The fruit of the Spirit is love, joy,
peace, patience, kindness, generosity,
faithfulness, gentleness, and self-control.
There is no law against such things.

GALATIANS CHAPTER 5, VERSE 16, GNB
AND VERSES 22–23, NRSV

A Changed Life

Whoever listens to the word but does not
put it into practice is like a man who
looks in a mirror and sees himself as he is.
He takes a good look at himself and then
goes away and at once forgets what he
looks like. But those who look closely into
the perfect law that sets people free, who
keep on paying attention to it and do not
simply listen and then forget it, but put it
into practice — they will be blessed by
God in what they do.

JAMES CHAPTER 1, VERSES 23–25, GNB

Love One Another

Dear friends, let us love one another, because love comes from God. Whoever loves is a child of God and knows God. Whoever does not love does not know God, for God is love. And God showed his love for us by sending his only Son into the world, so that we might have life through him. This is what love is: it is not that we have loved God, but that he loved us and sent his Son to be the means by which our sins are forgiven.

1 John chapter 4, verses 7–10, GNB

What Is Love?

Love is patient; love is kind; love is not envious or boastful or arrogant or rude. It does not insist on its own way; it is not irritable or resentful; it does not rejoice in wrongdoing, but rejoices in the truth. It bears all things, believes all things, hopes all things, endures all things.

Love never ends.

And now faith, hope, and love abide, these three; and the greatest of these is love.

1 Corinthians chapter 13, verses 4–8 and 13, NRSV

A World Made New

Jesus brought God's good news to a world that was spoiled by many bad things. Christians know that the world they live in is still full of evil and wrongdoing. They still die. Yet they firmly believe they will be safe with God forever. The time will come when God will put everything right. The last book of the Bible, Revelation, is a vision of the final great battle of Good and Evil and the victory of God through Jesus.

The Heavenly City

Then I saw a new heaven and a new earth; for the first heaven and the first earth had passed away, and the sea was no more. And I saw the holy city, the new Jerusalem, coming down out of heaven from God.

And I heard a loud voice from the throne saying,

"See, the home of God is among mortals.

He will dwell with them; they will be his people, and God himself will be with them;

he will wipe every tear from their eyes.

The Last Judgment

Then I saw a great white throne and the one who sat on it; the earth and the heaven fled from his presence, and no place was found for them. And I saw the dead, great and small, standing before the throne, and books were opened. Also another book was opened, the book of life. And the dead were judged according to their works, as recorded in the books.

REVELATION CHAPTER 20, VERSES 11–12, NRSV

Death will be no more; mourning and crying and pain will be no more, for the first things have passed away."

It [the city] has the glory of God and a radiance like a very rare jewel, like jasper, clear as crystal. It has a great, high wall with twelve gates . . . on the east three gates, on the north three gates, on the south three gates, and on the west three gates.

And the twelve gates are twelve pearls, each of the gates is a single pearl, and the street of the city is pure gold, transparent as glass.

REVELATION CHAPTER 21, VERSES 1–2; 3–4, 11–13 AND 21, NRSV

Jesus Will Come Soon

"See, I am coming soon; my reward is with me, to repay according to everyone's work. I am the Alpha and the Omega, the first and the last, the beginning and the end."

REVELATION CHAPTER 22, VERSES 12–13, NRSV

Index

Key to Bible Editions:

GNB = Good News Bible   **KJV** = Authorized King James Version
NRSV = New Revised Standard Version